I0060738

Women

DON'T GET LEFT BEHIND with

REAL ESTATE INVESTING

CHIQUITA LINDSAY

Copyright © 2020 by Chiquita Lindsay

All rights reserved. This book or any portion thereof may not be reproduced or used in any manner whatsoever without the express written permission of the publisher except for the use of brief quotations in a book review.

Jai Publishing House Incorporated
1230 Peachtree Street NE
19th Floor
Atlanta, Georgia 30309
www.jaipublishing.com

- DISCLAIMER -

This book does not provide a guarantee that you will get rich. This book is only a representation of how me and others have utilized Real Estate to retire early. Please consult a real estate or personal finance professional for the best results in executing the tactics in this book. Happy Retirement.

Printed in the United States of America

ISBN-13: 978-1-7352082-0-6

Comparative

agent

analysis Refinancing Listing

Adjustable-rate Assessed

value Closing Contingencies

Inspection reserves

Interest Appraisal Home

costs mortgage

market

Escrow broker Offer

Buyer's Dual Title Amortization

Equity Real

Fixed-rate Realtor

Cash warranty

Pre-approval

estate agency

insurance

letter Private

Listing

Introduction 1

The History of Women and Real Estate 8

The Current State of Women and Real Estate 14

Preparing for Real Estate Investing 24

Types of Real Estate Investing .. 28

Real Estate Investment Capital .. 38

Real Estate Investment Options. 52

Closing 68

About the Author 73

Introduction

It's amazing the things that you don't realize even though they're right under your nose. I worked for 38 years not realizing that REAL ESTATE was an opportunity for me to work for myself and not to have a job.

So even though I didn't really like my job, I went to work day in and day out hoping for something different but not really working towards a change.

It wasn't until I was determined to do something different and actually got some help to free me from my job that I realized REAL ESTATE was an opportunity for me to leave my job and work for myself.

My family never owned REAL ESTATE and I didn't inherit any property.

I convinced my husband that we needed to buy two properties in 2011, right in the middle of the housing bust.

Most people were getting out or losing REAL ESTATE at that time. I had an investor mindset even back then, but never thought about it as a career.

Property values were dropping and everything was on sale.

Women, we love a good sale, right?

My plan, at that time, was to have only two rentals, so that when my husband retired, his income wouldn't change.

I was thinking of HIM, and not realizing that REAL ESTATE would retire ME.

I always said "I couldn't afford" when the truth is, maybe I wasn't ready to sacrifice in order to change my life.

I bet even as you read this, you may have the opportunity to either earn more money or to spend less money so that you can invest in something like REAL ESTATE that will eventually free you—not only financially but also physically.

This book is going to challenge the way you look at your life, the way you look at your finances, and the way you look at your future.

I hope that you are open enough to see that even if you decide REAL ESTATE investing is not an option for you, you realize that as a woman you don't have to be left behind financially.

But unless you do something differently, you will be.

Love,

Chiquita

"

Most women want to be a REAL ESTATE agent. They only make a 6% commission off of each house they sell.

The 6% has to then be split in half with the buyer's agent. Now you're down to 3%, or less if you have to pay your broker.

A REAL ESTATE INVESTOR keeps 100% of the cash flow and 100% of the equity.

REAL ESTATE agents help investors get rich.

The History of Women and Real Estate

For a very long time (and not too long ago), women weren't even allowed to OWN land in their name. For example, if a father left his daughter some land, once she was married, that land became under the control of the husband.

Once women were able to own land in their own name, many times they weren't respected as "business owners" who had the same rights as men to run farms, own cattle, and buy even more land.

It's no wonder, based on our early history, that most women still feel that REAL ESTATE investment is for men.

Based on much of the gender bias in roles, many young girls are not taught about REAL ESTATE or don't even think of themselves as REAL ESTATE owners.

It is for this reason that many women are trapped in the past as it relates to REAL ESTATE investing and ownership.

APPRAISAL NO. 2

The Current State of
Women and Real
Estate

While women influence 91% of most REAL ESTATE buying decisions, only 25% are investors.

So why aren't more women investing? It is as simple as men and women process information differently.

MEN

- ▷ Tend to make decisions with more risks

- ▷ Make decisions to invest with very little information

- ▷ Driven by features

- ▷ See other people winning and want to win

WOMEN

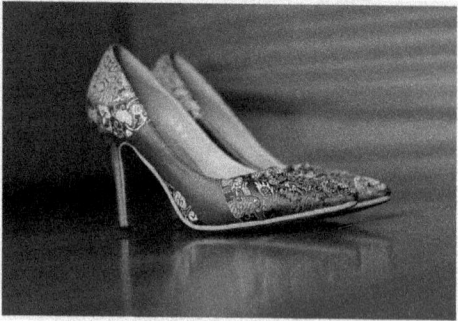

▷ Tend to play it more safe, less risks

▷ Need to hear the same information several times to make a decision

▷ Driven by emotions

▷ Want everyone to win

Although you may not like or agree with these differences, they are—for the most part—true.

So what do women need to do to change this?

🔑 LEARN TO CALCULATE RISK VS REWARD

As women we need to understand that although we may not invest with the same bravado and risky nature as men, it is imperative that we invest.

The REAL risk for women is getting left behind. Although women do 75% of the worlds work, we only own 10% of the world's wealth and 1% of the world's land.

🔑 EDUCATE THEMSELVES QUICKLY

The more we educate ourselves on the power of money and REAL ESTATE, the less we will be left behind.

Gone are the days that the family will be taken care of by the husband. Whether you never get married, get divorced after a year, or stay married to your husband for a thousand years, it is still your obligation, just as much as it is his, to protect the legacy of your family.

We can't sit by and wait on the information to come to us. We must progressively and aggressively pursue the information that will allow us to leave a legacy for ourselves, and for the ones we leave behind.

🗝 LESS EMOTIONS AND MORE BUSINESS

Women have to stop worrying so much about being wrong, and what everyone will think, versus making the decisions that are going to best prepare them for the future.

Instead of making decisions with our heart, we need to make decisions with our HEADS.

For example when it comes to collecting rent as a home owner. Women would be more prone to give the renter a chance to come up with the money, with the man being more business, would hold them to the contract and evict them if they couldn't pay.

By being more emotional as women, sometimes we put ourselves and our own finances at risk to do things to save others, not remembering there is no one to save us.

PUT THEMSELVES AND THEIR FUTURE FIRST

Women have to realize that the things we do TODAY are visited upon our future selves, good or bad. Now is time out for us to worry about the world, when so many women are landing in poverty.

It's not about being a bad person. It's about understanding that everyone in the world has the same opportunity to save themselves.

Just because they fail to take advantage of that opportunity, doesn't mean you follow them down the same rabbit hole to try to save them.

At some point we have to worry about our future selves and realize that we don't have as much control over life as we like.

Things happen. Owning your own REAL ESTATE is protection when they do.

Preparing for Real Estate Investing

REAL ESTATE Investing sometimes gets a BAD RAP as a get rich quick opportunity.

While the ability to generate a ton of revenue in REAL ESTATE is a great opportunity, you must know that JUST like anything else worth having, it is worth working for.

Don't think that you are going to go from working 8 hours a day at a job to working 1 day a week in REAL ESTATE.

In fact, because this IS your business, you may have to work EVEN harder to get it off the ground initially.

But keep that in mind.

🔑 This IS your business.

🔑 It is your security.

🔑 It is your legacy.

🔑 It is the future for you and your family.

Isn't THAT worth the hard work?

Types of Real
Estate Investing

There are two ways to get RICH in REAL ESTATE.

One is to **buy shares** of a REAL ESTATE investment trust.

In this example, you don't own the actual REAL ESTATE.

The type we prefer is **direct ownership**.

That means occupying, renting, flipping or wholesale.

The more you discuss REAL ESTATE the more you will come to know about each of these different ways to invest.

BUT WE ARE HERE TO DETERMINE IF YOU FIT THE BILL FOR INVESTING IN REAL ESTATE.

#1: *You are financially fit*

A lot of people get drawn into the no money down and the no credit needed trap of REAL ESTATE investing.

I am not saying those are not opportunities. But you have to be honest with yourself. If your financial instability is due to bad money management, then chances are you will still struggle when you invest in REAL ESTATE.

Make sure that you bring your good budgeting and money handling skills to the table.

#2: Do your homework

Many people want to instantly go from beginner to expert. It is important that you not jump the gun like that with real estate.

Read books and articles, attend real estate events, and more importantly consider hiring someone to help you along on your journey.

The money you spend hiring an expert is more often than not offset by the financial mistakes you may make without help; and the discouragement that comes from making mistakes.

#3: Invest based on your goals

Because each area of REAL ESTATE investment has the potential for vastly different long and short-term returns... make sure you invest!

#4: Have a plan

While experts may tell you to buy in neighborhoods where you would want to live, there are advantages to buy properties in other areas that may have future growth, future gentrification, or an influx of future business.

#5: Know Real Estate trends

The REAL ESTATE market tends to change from year to year.

By staying in a close-knit REAL ESTATE community of investors such as one you would find with a coach, you have the best bet of keeping up to date with trends AS they happen.

#6: You have good credit

Again, while this is not mandatory, it helps you improve your interest rates and how much money you are able to receive when your credit is favorable.

It is also a good litmus test that you will do what is required to make a success with your REAL ESTATE investments.

I teach many strategies that don't necessarily require you have good credit so if your credit is NOT quite ready and you are, make sure you contact us to ask.

#7: You have money in your retirement account or have received an inheritance to get started

Again, this is not mandatory and, in fact, in many of my classes I teach you how to get started with no money down.

However, we all know that SEED equal harvest and that the MORE you put in, the more you can expect to get out.

If you are ready to start REAL ESTATE investing SOONER rather than later, let's have a conversation on how you can get started EVEN if you don't measure up to everything on this list.

Sometimes being READY to do something different is enough to change your life.

We have convenient financing options with Low down payments available to help you create the BEST REAL ESTATE investment plan according to your life goals.

Real Estate
Investment Capital

Now that you may be convinced to invest in REAL ESTATE, you may be saying to yourself, "Where do I get the money to get started?"

We want to share with you some of the paths we have seen people take in the past.

However, we want to remind you that this is not a substitution for professional advice.

YOU are the best judge of your financial situation.

Also make sure you contact accountants and lawyers so that you can best protect your investments.

Remember, knowledge is power. The MORE you know about the REAL

ESTATE industry the more you can play it safe.

We have a variety of activities and courses to help you learn MORE about what properties may be the best investment for your region and overall.

Investment Capital Case Study A

If you are someone who formally needed a large home but now find yourself with MORE house than you need, converting your current home may be an option for you to get some capital to start investing in REAL ESTATE.

You can consider:

Buy a smaller home and rent your larger home out

Use the equity in your larger home to buy a smaller home and move to the smallest home, while renting the larger home out

Live in the downstairs of the larger home and rent the upstairs out in order to use the capital from the rent to invest in REAL ESTATE

Sell your larger home and use the proceeds to buy 2 or 3 small homes. Stay in one and rent the other 2.

None of these are a bad options, and the best option would depend mostly on what you prefer and the area of the country you live in.

Investment Capital Case Study B

☞ **CONVERTING YOUR RETIREMENT**

Depending on the rules for your retirement account you may be able to leverage your 401k to buy multiple properties to rent out.

This would be great for someone who may:

- ☑ Have no other way to come up with the capital

- ☑ Needs to aggressively catch up on their retirement

- ☑ Has quite a bit of funds in their retirement, but not quite enough for retirement.

Here's another case where you need to crunch the numbers, consult a professional, and do your homework.

Everything that sounds good is NOT good, but at the same time, if you know your retirement is trending behind it is best to do SOMETHING to try and help yourself, rather than sit by and do nothing.

Investment Capital Case Study C

Many people have more "extra money" than they give themselves credit for. You may want to start to track and save your discretionary income and start to get started with REAL ESTATE investment.

There are a variety of low and no money down programs that we can introduce to you that may help you get started soon rather than later.

Investment Capital Case Study D

With all of the employment flexibility nowadays, you may want to consider picking up additional hours or work an additional job until you get the income to start buying property.

Although this option may not seem ideal, you have to remember that not only is this a temporary option.

You are doing the work today to provide for your future. I am sure you would much rather work an extra job while you are 30 or 40, versus when you are 70 or 80.

Which is why you need to make sure you remember what you read in this book and NOT go back to a life without REAL ESTATE like you were living before.

If applied along with professional help, the knowledge you received in this book can save you. But it must be applied.

🏠 🏠 🏠

Investment Capital Case Study E

Don't rule out the idea of Improving your credit and leveraging Personal and Business Loans.

Most REAL ESTATE investors would rather leverage the capital from another company versus their personal resource.

The average household carried over $8k in debt. More than enough to get started with investing.

What if we changed our priorities from creating debt for our day to day wants and needs, to creating debt that would eventually pay for itself like REAL ESTATE.

Real Estate

Investment Options

Here are seven ways to invest in real estate that involve a purchase of actual property.

#1

BUY AND FIX UP A HOME

Mostly called Flip – You buy the home, fix it up, and sell it to someone for more.

Pro's ✅

You make more money in a shorter time window

Con's ⊠

Additional funds for fix up; requires knowledge of REAL ESTATE and home improvement

Mistakes to watch for: Be careful you don't spend MORE money on the flip and fixing it up that you have the potential to make in profits.

Otherwise you would have done all of that work for nothing.

I know they make it LOOK easy on TV, but this is not TV.

Ideally, anyway. Fixing a home requires funds beyond the initial investment, and more time than you might have.

It's a process, and one that requires a solid knowledge of REAL ESTATE and home improvement.

#2

RENT-TO-OWN A HOME

You sign a contract to rent the home with an intention to buy.

A percentage of your monthly rent payments go toward the down payment on a mortgage when the purchase becomes official.

Pro's ✅

Good for people who don't have the credit to buy a home.

Con's ❌

Make sure you are comfortable with the home on a long-term basis, because eventually it will be yours. Read your contract carefully and ask questions.

#|3

BECOME A LANDLORD

You can either buy a property and rent out rooms or apartments or rent out rooms in your own home.

Pro's ✅

You have other's contributing to your investment

Con's 🅇

Being a landlord can be tricky. Make sure you learn the laws in what to look out for.

We have a course that helps you understand the best ways not to get stuck holding the rent check.

#️⃣4

PURCHASE VACATION PROPERTY

Vacation property means renting out to tenants for shorter periods. Maintain a good house in the right area, and you may be able to make the same money off a few vacation tenants that you might make from a year-round tenant elsewhere.

VACATION RENTALS

Purchasing an additional home in a desirable vacation area

Pro's ✅

Gives you flexibility on where you live, especially if retired

Con's ❌

Can be expensive to buy and maintain. You also have to consider off seasons, such as beach properties that may remain mostly empty during the winter season.

5

USE LODGING APPS LIKE AIRBNB

Renting your home like a hotel

Pro's ✅

Great for cities that have annual regional events (like the Kentucky Derby or Indy 500) or once in a few years events (like Superbowl or NBA All star)

Con's ☒

Everyone is not going to treat your home like you do. Know how to ensure guests follow the rules and what your recourse is if they cause damage.

#6

PURCHASE COMMERCIAL, NON-RESIDENTIAL PROPERTY

The purchase of office buildings and non-residential property

Pro's ✅

Can lead to bigger investment rewards

Con's ❌

Can also be more costly to start and also lead to more costly losses

You may want to bring in several partners for a venture of this magnitude and again, make sure you KNOW what you are doing before you go this big.

#7

YOUR OWN HOUSE!

Yes, if you bought a house and now live in it, congrats. You're a real-estate investor!

Pro's ✅

You are not WASTING money on rent. Each payment is towards something that will eventually belong to you.

Con's ❎

Because it does belong to you, there is no one to call when the garbage disposal breaks.

Make sure you keep good handy men
and a few dollars on hand for when
things need to be repaired.

🏠

For more works by Chiquita
Lindsay, visit chiquitalindsay.com

🏠

APPRAISAL NO. 7

Closing

REAL ESTATE Investing is often misunderstood as a get rich quick opportunity.

While the ability to generate a ton of revenue in REAL ESTATE is a great opportunity, you must know that JUST like anything else worth having, it is worth working for.

Don't think that you are going to go from working 8 hours a day at a job to working 1 day a week in REAL ESTATE.

In fact, because this IS your business, you may have to work EVEN harder to get it off the ground initially.

But keep that in mind. This IS your business. It is your security. It is your legacy. It is the future for you and your family. Isn't THAT worth the hard work?

Also regardless as to what you SEE on TV, watching episodes of Flip this house doesn't qualify you to go out and start REAL ESTATE investment.

You need a behind the scenes education in making this work.

Consider attending one of our live auctions or one of our courses to make sure that you get an understanding of what is really required as you start your journey towards becoming a REAL ESTATE investor.

So that you can do this RIGHT and don't have to worry about being LEFT behind!

Let's Build Shall We!

About the Author

CHIQUITA LINDSAY is an author, speaker, expert REAL ESTATE investor and coach with 10 plus years of experience as a certified landlord coach.

Chiquita is a professional flipper, wholesaler, and owner of several rental properties. She specializes in all things on the investment side real estate.

Chiquita was featured in Courageous Magazine and served as a real estate editor for Exposure Online Magazine.

She is the founder of Stop Working Broke Bootcamp and served as president of the KY Chapter of Wealthy Sisters Network.

Chiquita is the author of Amazon Best Seller, "Quit Affirmations."

She resides in Louisville, KY, she's married with young adult children and a caretaker of her elderly mother.

Her mission is to help women build a Queendom and leave a legacy for their families by owning land and investing in real estate.

Follow Chiquita on Periscope @gclindsay and @StopWorkingBrok

www.ingramcontent.com/pod-product-compliance
Lightning Source LLC
Chambersburg PA
CBHW060643210326
41520CB00010B/1716